Time for Bed

Bible Stories

Time for Bed Bible Stories
Written by Juliet David
Illustrated by Sarah Pitt

Distributed in the UK by Marston Book Services Ltd,
PO Box 269, Abingdon, Oxon OX14 4YN

Distributed in the USA by Kregel Publications,
PO Box 2607, Grand Rapids, Michigan 49501

Worldwide co-edition produced by Lion Hudson plc,
Wilkinson House, Jordan Hill Road, Oxford OX2 8DR
Tel: +44 (0)1865 302750 Fax: +44 (0)1865 302757
Email: coed@lionhudson.com

ISBN 978 1 85985 778 6

Printed in December 2009,
by Star Standard Industries, Singapore

Time for Bed

Bible Stories

by Juliet David

illustrated by Sarah Pitt

CANDLE
BOOKS

Contents

Noah Builds an Ark

Hammer, hammer, hammer! Saw, saw, saw!
Noah is building a great big ark.
God told him, "A great flood is coming. Build an ark to save your family from the flood."

Noah's friends think he's mad – building an ark on dry land.

God tells Noah, "Collect two of every kind of animal.
Then march them into the ark."

So Noah leads the animals into the ark, two by two.
Two lions, two elephants, two giraffes, two mice, two tortoises.
Two of every sort of creature.

God shuts the door of the ark. Then the rain comes. Soon the ark is floating on the water. Noah, his family and the animals are all safe inside. There is plenty of food for Noah's family and for the animals too.

At last – after forty days – the rain stops. The water starts to go down. Noah wants to know if land has appeared. So he sends out a dove. It flies back with a leaf in its beak. There must be trees above water. And dry land!

Crash! The ark has landed. Noah opens the door. Out march all the animals – two lions, two elephants, two giraffes, two mice, two tortoises. Noah and his family come out too.
God puts a beautiful rainbow in the sky.
"I will never again flood all the earth," he promises.

Jacob's Dream

Isaac and Rebekah had twin sons. Esau, the first twin, was very hairy. He loved to go hunting. Isaac loved him more than his brother.

But Jacob, the other twin, liked to stay at home with his mother. He was full of tricks. Rebekah loved him more.

One day, Jacob stole from his brother Esau.
Esau was furious. So Jacob had to run away from home.

One night Jacob lay down all alone to sleep in the desert.
He used a stone as his pillow.

Jacob had a wonderful dream. He saw a stairway to heaven.
Angels walked up and down.

When Jacob woke up next morning he said,
"God is here with me!"

Joseph and his Special Coat

Jacob had a very big family. Altogether he had twelve sons.
But Jacob loved Joseph more than all his other sons.
He gave Joseph a wonderful coat.

One day Joseph told his brothers, "I've had a dream. It was harvest time. We all had bundles of grain. Your bundles of grain bowed to mine!"

"So you think we should bow down to *you?*" said his brothers. They were so angry that they threw Joseph down a hole in the ground.

Then they sold Joseph to traders.
But the brothers told old Jacob, "Joseph has been killed by
a wild animal."

The traders took Joseph to the far-off land of Egypt.

After many adventures, the king of Egypt put Joseph in charge of his country. And one day Joseph's father and brothers came to live in Egypt too.

The Baby in the Basket

"There are too many Israelites," said the king of Egypt.
"Throw every Israelite baby boy into the river."

One Israelite mother wanted to keep her baby boy safe.
She made a plan. "We'll hide baby in a basket," she told her
daughter, Miriam.

They floated the basket among the reeds.
"Hide and watch what happens," said Miriam's mother.

The princess of Egypt came to bathe.
"Whatever's that?" she asked.
Her maid lifted the basket from the water.
"What a beautiful baby!" gasped the princess.

Miriam was watching.

"Princess, do you need a nurse for the baby?" she asked.

"Yes please!" said the princess. So Miriam ran home.

"Mother!" she called. "The princess needs someone to look after baby." They raced back to the river.

"Princess," said Miriam's mother. "Would you like me to nurse the baby?"

"Yes," said the princess. "Let's call him 'Moses'. When he's older, he shall come to live with me."

And Moses was brought up as a prince in the royal palace.

David and the Giant

God sent old Samuel to choose a new king of Israel. He went to the home of a man called Jesse and looked at his seven sons. "Do you have any more sons?" Samuel asked.

"There is my youngest son, David," said Jesse.
"He's minding the sheep."
"He is the one who shall be king," God told Samuel.

God made David brave and strong. One day David went to see his brothers, who were soldiers. They were all afraid of a giant named Goliath.

But David wasn't frightened. He took five little stones and his sling and went to fight Goliath.

The giant laughed when he saw David was just a boy.
But David threw a stone. It hit Goliath on the head and killed him.

30

Daniel and the Lions

Darius the Great was King of the Medes and the Persians. One day he chose Daniel to be his top wise man. Daniel prayed to God every morning, lunchtime and night.

But the other wise men were jealous of Daniel.
"O king," they said. "Make a new law: no one must pray except
to you. Anyone who breaks this law shall be thrown to the lions."

Then they hid outside Daniel's house to spy on him.

They rushed back to the palace.
"O king!" they said sneakily. "We've seen Daniel praying to his God. Throw him to the lions!"

Darius was very sorry because he liked Daniel.
But soldiers grabbed Daniel and threw him to the lions.

Next morning, Darius hurried to the lion pit.
There stood Daniel. "An angel shut the lions' mouths
so they couldn't hurt me," said Daniel.
Darius was so happy!

Jonah and the Gigantic Man-swallowing Fish

"Go to the city of Nineveh!" God said to Jonah one day.
"Tell the people there to turn their lives around."
But Jonah ran off and jumped aboard a ship!

God sent a wild storm. The sailors were scared silly.

Jonah told the sailors, "It's all my fault. I didn't do what God told me. Throw me into the sea!" So the sailors flung Jonah into the sea – and the storm stopped at once.

Suddenly a huge, enormous fish swam up and swallowed Jonah.
Jonah prayed from the fish's tummy: "Lord, please save me!"

God heard Jonah. The fish spat him out on the seashore.
God told Jonah again: "Go to Nineveh!"
This time Jonah did as God said.

The First Christmas

Mary lived in a little village called Nazareth.
She was going to marry Joseph the carpenter.

One day Mary had a surprise. An angel appeared!
"Don't be scared, Mary," said the angel. "I have good news.
You're going to have a baby. Call him Jesus."

Joseph and Mary had to go to the town of Bethlehem.
It was a long way and they both grew tired.
At last they saw the town in the distance.

When they arrived, all the houses were full. One man saw Mary's tired face. "You can stay in my stable," he said. So they did.

There in his stable, baby Jesus was born. The cows and horses watched. The newborn baby slept. How happy Mary was!

The Visitors' Story

In fields nearby, shepherds were minding their flocks. Suddenly an angel appeared. "Baby Jesus is born in Bethlehem," he said. Then a crowd of angels appeared, singing at the top of their voices.

The shepherds left their sheep and rushed off to find baby Jesus.
When they came to the stable, they knelt before him.

Far, far away, some wise men saw a special new star.
"That means a new king has been born," said one.

The wise men journeyed miles and miles to find baby Jesus, the newborn king. They brought rich gifts for him: gold, frankincense and myrrh.

Lost in the Temple

Mary and Joseph took Jesus back home to Nazareth. Jesus grew up there. He helped his parents and played with his friends.

When Jesus was twelve, Mary and Joseph took him to Jerusalem for a special festival. But they lost Jesus in the crowds.

Mary and Joseph searched everywhere for Jesus. At last they found him in the temple talking to some teachers. They thought he was very wise.

"Jesus, why did you stay here?" Mary asked. "We were worried about you."

Jesus said, "I had to do my heavenly Father's work!"

At home in Nazareth, Jesus helped Joseph the carpenter.
But he knew God had a very special job for him to do.

Follow Me!

One day, Jesus saw four fishermen mending their fishing nets beside the lake. They were named:

Peter,

Andrew,

James

and John.

"Follow me," said Jesus. "And I will teach you to catch men instead of fish!"

All four left their boats and became Jesus' friends.

Jesus Calms a Storm

One day Jesus was sailing across the lake
with his special friends,
the disciples.

He was very tired
and fell fast asleep.

Suddenly a great storm arose. The boat started to fill with water. The disciples felt very frightened. They shook Jesus awake. "Help us, Master!" they said.

Jesus stood up and said,

"Storm, be still!"

At once, everything was quiet again. The disciples were amazed!
Even the wind and the waves listened to Jesus.

Jesus Feeds a Great Crowd

One day Jesus was telling people stories in the country. They listened all day. By evening, they were very hungry.

Nobody had any food except one boy.
He had five loaves and two fish.
The boy gave them to Jesus.

Jesus' friends gave out the food. There were five thousand
people – but there was enough food for everyone!

There were even twelve baskets full of leftovers.
People were amazed at this miracle that Jesus did.

The Story of the Good Shepherd

Jesus told many great stories. They had a special, secret meaning. Here are two of them.

There was once a shepherd who had one hundred sheep.

One sheep went missing.

At once, the shepherd went to search for it.

Where could it be? He searched everywhere for his lost sheep.

At last the shepherd found his lost sheep.
He put it gently on his shoulders and carried it home.

"Come to my party," the shepherd told his friends.
"I've found my lost sheep!"
Jesus said, "God is happy too when anyone comes to him."

The Story of the Lost Son

Jesus told a story about a man who had two sons.
One day the younger son decided to leave home.

He went far away and gave lots of parties.
But one day he found he had no money left.

Now the son had to work. He looked after pigs.
He was so hungry that he even ate the pigs' food.

At last, the younger son decided to return home.

His father was very happy when his son arrived home.

He even threw a party to celebrate.

Jesus Helps Jairus's Daughter

A man called Jairus had a dear little girl.

One day she became very ill. The doctors couldn't do anything for her, so Jairus ran to fetch Jesus. He wanted Jesus to help.

But when Jesus arrived, the little girl had already died. Jesus said to her, "Wake up, my dear!" She got up and had something to eat. Jesus had done another miracle!

Jesus and the Children

One day some mothers wanted to bring their children to meet Jesus.

"Go away!" said the disciples.
"Jesus is much too tired to talk to children!"

But Jesus heard them. "Let the children come to me," he said. "No one gets into God's kingdom unless they come like a child."

Jesus and the Tiny Taxman

One day Jesus visited a town where there lived a tiny man called Zacchaeus. He collected taxes. No one liked him because he took too much money.

Zacchaeus wanted to see Jesus, but he was too short.

So he climbed a tree.

Jesus saw him up the tree.
"Climb down, Zacchaeus!" said Jesus.
"I want to come and see you."

Zacchaeus changed completely after he met Jesus.
He even gave back all the money he had taken.

Palm Sunday

One day Jesus and his friends went to Jerusalem for a festival. On the way Jesus said, "Go and find a young donkey. Bring it to me."

Jesus' friends came back with a donkey. They spread their coats on its back. Then Jesus climbed on the donkey.

The donkey went clip-clop down the road. People threw down coats for the donkey to walk on. They took palm branches and waved them. "Praise God!" they shouted.

People Plot against Jesus

But some people in Jerusalem hated Jesus.
They wanted to kill him.

Some of these people took Jesus to the ruler.
He said, "Jesus hasn't done anything wrong."
But people shouted, "Kill him! Kill him!"

So soldiers took Jesus and put him on a wooden cross.
They left him to die. Jesus' followers were terribly sad.
They had lost a very special friend.

Jesus is Alive!

Jesus' friends buried him in a cave.
They rolled a huge stone across its doorway.

After three days they came back.
The stone had been rolled away!

Two angels were inside the cave.
"Don't be frightened," said the angels.
"Jesus is alive! He has risen from the dead!"